From Sole to Sold **by Jill Hills and Attorney Mark Nicholson**

Copyright © 2024 by Jill Hills and Mark Nicholson

All rights reserved.

No portion of this book may be reproduced in any form without written permission from the publisher or author, except as permitted by U.S. copyright law.

ISBN: 9798344584072

Table of Contents

Chapter One 5
Chapter Two 11
Chapter Three 36
Chapter Four 41
Chapter Five 47
Chapter Six 54
Chapter Seven 69
Chapter Eight 74
Chapter Nine 80
Chapter Ten 88
Chapter Eleven 91

Foreword

This book is designed to provide valuable insights and practical tips for women looking to enter the lucrative market of selling feet pictures online. Selling feet pictures has become a popular and profitable business venture for many individuals, and this book aims to guide you through the process of setting up and running a successful feet picture business.

One of the key aspects covered in this book is how to sell feet pictures effectively. You will learn how to attract and retain a loyal customer base, from pricing strategies to customer engagement techniques. Additionally, we will discuss the importance of creating high-quality feet pictures that are visually appealing and marketable to potential buyers.

Setting up a successful feet picture business requires more than just taking a few photos and posting them online. In this book, we will delve into the various platforms available for selling feet pictures, as well as the legal considerations that you need to be aware of before getting started. Equally important is building a brand for selling feet pictures. We will provide expert advice on creating a unique and memorable brand that stands out in the crowded online marketplace, a key factor in your business's success.

 Marketing strategies are another important aspect of selling feet pictures online, and we will explore different techniques for promoting your products and reaching a wider audience. Whether you are new to the business or looking to expand your existing feet picture business, this book will equip you with the knowledge and tools needed to succeed in this competitive industry.

Overall, "From Sole to Sold: Platforms for Selling Feet Pictures Online" is a comprehensive guide for women interested in tapping into the profitable market of selling feet pictures online.

Following the tips and strategies outlined in this book, you can build a successful feet picture business and earn a lucrative income from your passion for foot photography.

Disclaimer: Some of the names, places, and events have been changed to protect the innocent and guilty and their privacy.

Chapter One

Getting Started with Selling Feet Pictures

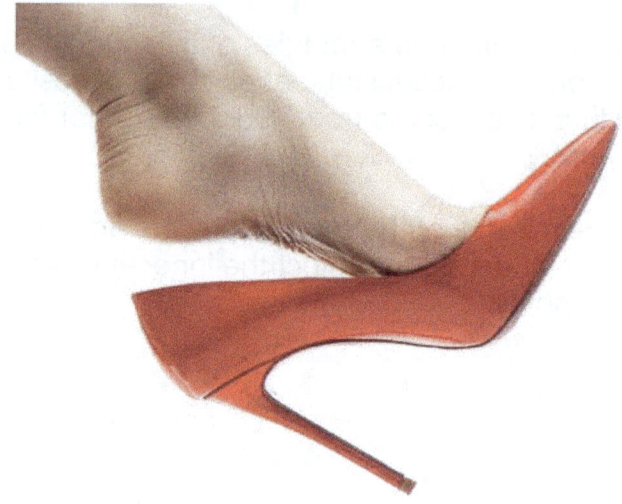

Understanding the market for feet pictures is essential for anyone looking to sell their own pictures online. In today's digital age, the demand for feet pictures has skyrocketed, with many individuals willing to pay top dollar for high-quality images. Women, especially female models, have a unique opportunity to capitalize on this growing market and turn their feet into a profitable business.

When selling feet pictures, it's essential to understand the various platforms available for showcasing and selling your images. From dedicated feet picture websites like and to social media platforms like Instagram and Twitter, there are countless ways to reach potential buyers and build a successful business. By utilizing these platforms effectively, women can attract a large audience of foot fetishists and maximize their earning potential.

In addition to choosing the right platforms for selling feet pictures, it's crucial to consider legal considerations when entering this niche market. Understanding copyright laws, privacy issues, and other potential legal pitfalls can help protect your business and ensure a smooth selling process. By staying informed and following best practices, women can confidently navigate the legal landscape of selling feet pictures.

Building a brand for selling feet pictures is another key aspect of success in this market. By developing a unique identity and style for your images, you can stand out from the competition and attract a loyal following of customers. Whether you focus on artistic shots, fetish-themed content, or something in between, creating a recognizable brand can help you become a top seller in the feet picture market.

Ultimately, creating high-quality feet pictures is the foundation of a successful business in this niche. By investing in professional equipment, mastering photography techniques, and honing your editing skills, you can produce quality images that command top dollar from buyers. With a focus on quality and consistency, women can build a thriving business selling feet pictures and capitalize on the lucrative market for foot fetish content.

Why Women are...

Successful in Selling Feet Pictures

Women have been incredibly successful in the business of selling feet pictures for a variety of reasons. One of the main factors is that women often have a keen understanding of what sells in the market. They can tap into the desires and preferences of their target audience (mainly men), which allows them to create highly sought-after content. Additionally, women are often more adept at marketing themselves and their products. They understand the power of branding and know how to make a solid and appealing online presence that attracts customers.

Furthermore, traditionally, viewing almost any part of a woman's body can attract men and their money. In a society that places a high value on physical appearance, women can leverage their natural (and sometimes fake) assets to their advantage. Female models, in particular, have a unique ability to create stunning and alluring images that captivate their audience and drive sales. Their experience in front of the camera gives them a distinct advantage when creating high-quality feet pictures that are in demand.

In addition to their marketing and branding skills, women excel at building customer relationships. They understand the importance of customer service and can cultivate a loyal following of repeat buyers. Women can establish trust and credibility in the industry by engaging with their audience personally and providing excellent customer care. This, in turn, leads to increased sales and a steady income stream.

Regarding legal considerations, people should contact an attorney to ensure compliance with all relevant laws and regulations. Understanding the importance of protecting your intellectual property rights and taking the necessary steps to safeguard your work product is essential. By staying informed about copyright laws and licensing agreements, models can protect their business and avoid potential legal and personal issues that could arise from selling feet pictures online.

Overall, female models have proven to be highly successful in the business of selling feet pictures due to men being the primary consumers of this fetish. An article in Psychology Today said foot fetishes are one of the most common fetishes. Below is the percentage of people who have been estimated to have a foot fetish.

- 5% of heterosexual women
- 18% of heterosexual men
- 11% of lesbian and bisexual women
- 21% of gay and bisexual men.

By leveraging your marketing, branding, customer care, and legal compliance strengths, you can establish a thriving business that caters to a niche market of foot fetish enthusiasts. With the right strategies and platforms, you can turn people's passion for feet pictures into a lucrative and sustainable source of income.

Overcoming Taboos and Stigmas Associated with Selling Feet Pictures

In the world of online entrepreneurship, one niche that has gained popularity in recent years is selling feet pictures. However, this industry is often shrouded in taboos and stigmas that can make it difficult to break into. Overcoming these taboos and stigmas is crucial for success in the business of selling feet pictures.

One of the first steps to overcoming taboos and stigmas associated with selling feet pictures is to educate oneself on the industry and its potential for success. By understanding the demand for feet pictures and the market for them, women can feel more confident in their decision to enter this niche. Additionally, educating oneself on the legal considerations for selling feet pictures can help alleviate any concerns about the legality of this business.

Another important aspect of overcoming taboos and stigmas is building an authentic and professional brand. By creating a strong brand identity and marketing strategy, women can position themselves as experts in the field of selling foot pictures. This can help dispel any negative stereotypes or misconceptions about the industry and establish credibility with potential customers.

Creating high-quality feet pictures is also essential for overcoming taboos and stigmas associated with selling feet pictures. By investing in professional photography equipment and mastering the art of capturing stunning images of their feet, women can set themselves apart from competitors and attract a loyal customer base. High-quality photos can also normalize the practice of selling feet pictures and showcase the beauty and artistry of this niche. However, investing in professional photography equipment is not a must. The quality of cellphone cameras is such that you can still make money just by using the camera on your phone. An often overlooked skill in photography is lighting. Using proper lighting techniques can turn an okay picture into a great one.

Ultimately, overcoming taboos and stigmas associated with learning to sell feet pics requires confidence, education, and professionalism. By building a strong brand, creating high-quality images, and educating oneself on the industry's legal considerations, women can successfully navigate the challenges of this niche and establish a thriving business selling feet pictures online.

Chapter Two

Jill Hills Sells

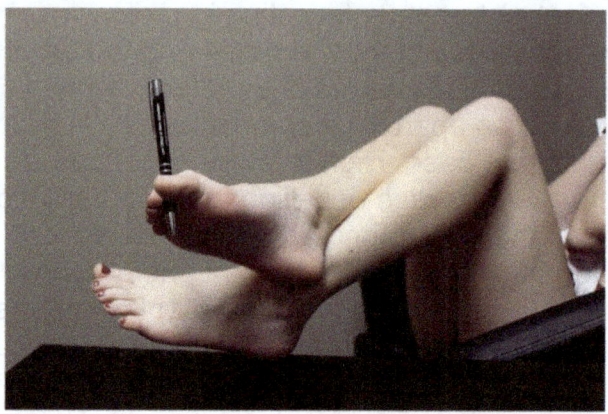

My journey into the foot modeling world began quite unexpectedly when I was a teenager. One summer day, while wearing sandals, an older man complimented my feet, saying they were cute. At first, I didn't think much about it, but that comment planted a seed in my head.

Early Beginnings

Growing up, I never considered my feet anything special. However, that single compliment made me start paying attention to them and realize their potential. Soon after, I started taking better care of my feet - trimming my nails regularly, using moisturizer, and even getting pedicures occasionally.

I wanted to ensure they were always in top condition.

Suddenly, my friends would ask where I got my nail polish from or what products I used to keep my feet looking so soft and smooth. Some would tease me about having model-worthy feet and beg for tips on making theirs look half as good.

I worked at a local thrift store during my senior year of high school. A frequent customer named Mr. Johnson came in at least once a week. Mr. Johnson was an older Black man, likely in his 60s, with a bald head and kind eyes that crinkled at the corners when he smiled. His face showed a life well-lived, with weathered and lined features. He always dressed in a crisp shirt and slacks and polished his shoes immaculately to a shine every time. He complimented me on my feet. Whenever I wore sandals or something that allowed my feet to show, he would say something about them.

"I like the color of your toenail polish," he said. Or, "Did you get a pedicure recently? Because your feet look fantastic."

I usually responded with a "Thank you, Mr. Johnson." Then he would smile at me with his straight white teeth. His teeth were a perfect row of ivory, each one like a tiny white pearl nestled in its own bed of pink gum, surrounded by his thick lips. They were always displayed when he smiled, a dazzling contrast to the weathered wrinkles on his dark black face.

The first time he saw my feet, he alluded to my arches. I can't remember exactly what he said, but I know it was some indirect comment about my arches. I have very high arches. With a pronounced curve, my arch creates a gap between the ball of my foot and the ground, making it truly unique. They are like perfect crescents that perfectly frame my slender toes.

As a child, I didn't recognize myself as having high arches. I just thought my arches were normal. That is, until middle school when the older man saw my sandaled feet.

Now, returning to the old Black male customer at the thrift shop. The chime above the thrift store door heralded his arrival. I glanced up from my task of aligning mismatched shoes on an aged wooden shelf and found myself caught in the warm smile of Mr. Harold Johnson.

"Good afternoon, Jill," he greeted me, his soft baritone voice vibrating gently through the air.

"Hello, Mr. Johnson," I replied, feeling the corners of my own mouth lifting in response to his unwavering cheerfulness. "Back for another treasure hunt?"

"Indeed," he said, his dark eyes twinkling with childlike excitement that belied his years. Mr. Johnson always dressed as though he had stepped out of a refined era long passed—one where men wore hats unironically and polished their shoes with religious fervor. Today was no exception; a tweed jacket embraced his shoulders, perfectly complementing the crispness of his cream-colored shirt.

"Perhaps you can point me toward your latest

arrivals?" he inquired politely, his hands clasped neatly behind his back.

"Of course," I said, gesturing toward a rack of freshly donated clothing. "We just received some vintage suits that you might like."

As we walked, the subtle scent of sandalwood and old paper emanated from him, mingling with the musty, comforting smell perpetually hanging about the shop like a faithful ghost. It was soothing—the olfactory equivalent of a sepia-toned photograph.

"Thank you, my dear," Mr. Johnson said, pausing to examine a particularly well-preserved blazer. His appreciation for the garment was palpable as if he could read its history with a single touch.

Then, as I stood by patiently, his gaze dropped to my feet, encased in simple sandals that were practical for a day's work yet revealed more than they concealed. The comment emerged from his lips with the ease and naturalness of any other compliment: "You know, Jill, you have quite elegant feet. Very striking arches and slender toes."

The unexpected and intimate words brushed against my consciousness like the delicate wings of a moth seeking light. For a split second, time seemed to slow, and I felt the weight of his gaze like a physical touch upon my skin—a caress that echoed with a peculiar intimacy.

"Thank—thank you," I stammered, suddenly conscious of the bareness of my feet beneath his discerning eye. A blush crept up my neck, unfurling like the petals of a timid flower under the sun's insistent coaxing.

"Forgive me if I've overstepped," Mr. Johnson added quickly, noting my reaction. "It's just that, in my line of work, I've learned to notice beauty where others might overlook it."

His reassurance was gentle, like a soothing balm, and I found myself offering a small, genuine smile despite the fluttering in my chest. "No offense taken," I assured him, finding a certain pride swelling within at the notion that there might be beauty in something so mundane as my own feet.

"Very good, then." He returned his attention to the clothes before us, but the air between us remained tinged with the echo of his words.

The rest of our interaction unfolded with the usual pleasantries, but beneath the surface of our conversation, my mind whirled with newfound curiosity. Could there truly be an artistry to the arch of a foot, the length of a toe?

Mr. Johnson left with a vintage suit under his arm and another warm smile, leaving me to ponder the potential that lay hidden in the very foundation of my being—my feet. In the quiet aftermath of his departure, I felt the seeds of possibility taking root, whispering of paths untrodden and horizons yet unseen.

Later that evening, in the privacy of my bedroom, I hesitated before a full-length mirror. Mr. Johnson's words had lingered, and now they beckoned me to examine what I'd always taken for granted: my own feet.

I slipped off my sandals, a ritual of revelation, and placed one foot then the other upon a stool, tilting my head as I considered them. High arches, indeed, creating shadowed valleys beneath my ankles. My toes, slender and uniform, stretched outward with an almost ballerina's grace. Were these really the unnoticed features Mr. Johnson had admired?

"Curious," I murmured to myself, tracing the curve of my instep with a fingertip and marveling at the smoothness of my skin. A sense of wonder washed over me and, with it, a burgeoning affection for these overlooked appendages.

In the days that followed, my routine began to transform. Where I once regarded foot care as a mere necessity, I now approach it with the precision of an artist tending to her masterpiece.
Each evening became a sacred ritual: warm soaks in scented water, gentle exfoliation, and meticulous trimming. I learned to moisturize with careful attention, massaging rich creams into every contour until my skin felt like satin.

I experimented with nail polishes, selecting hues that complimented my skin tone, and took time to perfect the art of the pedicure. The sight of my feet adorned with glossy color brought an unexpected thrill—a secret delight in their newfound beauty.

In moments of solitude, I would stretch and flex my feet, observing how the muscles moved and how the bones aligned. With each passing day, my confidence grew. These were no longer just the tools that carried me from place to place; they were a part of me, unique and beautiful in their form.

It was a peculiar thing to find such fascination with a part of myself I had so long ignored, but Mr. Johnson's offhand compliment had sparked something within me. A fire of self-appreciation, a desire to care for and cherish every aspect of who I was—even down to the very tips of my toes.

As I sat there each night, attending to my feet with newfound reverence, I couldn't help but wonder if this small act of self-care might be the first step toward a future I had never dared to imagine.

After several months of complimenting my feet, I noticed he gave me tips. If I wore shoes showcasing my feet, he would tip me. It seemed like the more my feet showed, the bigger the tip.

Despite the strange attention and increasing tips from the customer at the thrift shop, I couldn't deny the thrill of his compliments about my feet. It was as if he saw something in them I had never noticed before. With each passing week, I eagerly anticipated his visits, wondering what new compliment or tip he would offer next. Yes, I specifically wore sandals to show off my feet and get a tip.

The thrift store, a kaleidoscope of past fashions and forgotten stories, hummed with the quiet energy of the afternoon rush. Amidst the organized chaos, my hands glided over the worn spines of vintage books and smoothed out creases from donated dresses that whispered secrets of bygone eras. My mind, however, was awash in a sea of doubt and trepidation, fingers absentmindedly tracing the soft leather of an abandoned pair of ballet flats.

"Jill, you've got this thoughtful look again," Maria observed earlier that day during lunch, her brow furrowing in concern under the shade of the school's old oak tree. "What's brewing up there?"

I smiled, brushing off her curiosity with a shrug, but the question lingered, echoing in the hollow spaces between the racks of clothes. Could I really pursue foot modeling? The very thought sent ripples through the calm surface of my once-predictable life.

"Beautiful selection today, Jill." Mr. Johnson's rich and comforting voice pulled me back to the present as he approached the counter with a small pile of silk ties. You have quite the eye for color coordination."

"Thank you, Mr. Johnson," I replied, cheeks warming under his praise as I rang up his finds. His presence was like a gentle tide, coaxing me further into uncharted waters each time he visited.

His smile widened, eyes glancing downward briefly before meeting mine again. "And how are those splendid feet of yours? Still treating them like royalty, I hope."

I couldn't help but laugh, sounding more nervous than I intended. "Of course. It's kind of become a routine now," I said, tucking a stray lock of hair behind my ear. I felt the weight of his gaze like a physical touch.

"Good, good," he nodded approvingly. "Talent should always be nurtured."

My heart fluttered at his words—talent? Was that truly what lay within the graceful curves of my arches, the delicate lines of my toes?

As I handed him his change and watched him leave, his parting compliment lingering in the air like a rare perfume, I felt the pull of possibility tugging at me. Was I ready to step into this new role, to bare a part of myself to the world in such an intimate way?

The bell above the door jingled softly as another customer entered, breaking the spell. But the seed of uncertainty had been planted, roots twining around my resolve.

"Embrace your uniqueness, Jill," I murmured to myself, recalling the affirmation from the night before. Yet embracing was one thing; revealing was another altogether.

Even as the sun dipped lower, casting slanted beams of golden light through the storefront window, my thoughts circled back to Mr. Johnson's visits and his encouraging words, which seemed to see something in me I was still struggling to acknowledge.

"Could I really do it?" The question hung suspended in the twilight of the thrift store, unanswered but alive with the potential that tomorrow might hold the key to unlocking the door to a world I never imagined stepping into.

As our interactions became more frequent, he eventually broached the topic of foot modeling. The chime of the thrift store door announced his arrival. I looked up, my heart skipping a beat as Mr. Johnson strode in, his presence commanding yet comforting. As he approached, I felt the now-familiar flutter of anticipation. What words would he grace me with today?

"Good afternoon, Jill," he greeted, his voice smooth as silk. He placed an old desk lamp on the counter; the pattern of colors was vibrant against the worn wood. I trust you're doing well?"

"Hi, Mr. Johnson," I replied, a small smile playing on my lips. "Yes, thank you. And yourself?"

"Quite well, quite well indeed," he said, his gaze drifting down to my feet clad in simple sandal flats. My breath caught slightly, knowing what often followed his contemplative look.

"Jill, have you ever considered... foot modeling?" The question hung in the air, as unexpected as a cold breeze in the midst of summer's heat. His eyes met mine, earnest and encouraging.

"Foot modeling?" I echoed, my surprise evident. The idea seemed to hover around me like a butterfly, elusive and delicate.

"Indeed," he continued, leaning forward slightly. "Your feet, with their high arches and slender toes, they possess a unique beauty. The industry would value such distinct features."

I blinked, feeling a twinge of vulnerability. The thought of exposing my feet to unknown eyes sparked an internal conflict. It was one thing for Mr. Johnson, with his fatherly warmth, to appreciate them, but to step into the limelight?

"I'm not sure," I murmured, my fingers tracing the edge of the wooden countertop. "It's not something I've ever really thought about."

"Of course, it's not a decision to be taken lightly," he acknowledged, his tone gentle. "But consider it, Jill. You might find a new aspect of yourself that you never knew existed."

He handed me a business card with his name on it. "Give me a call," he said with a smile. "You never know where your feet might take you."

His words lingered, wrapping around me like a protective and provocative shawl. As he left, his usual compliment absent but replaced with something far more potent, I was left with a tingling sense of curiosity.

Closing time found me alone with the hum of fluorescent lights and the echo of my own thoughts. Mr. Johnson's business card felt heavy with potential as it lay in my palm. I turned it over, and the number printed there seemed to pulse with the invitation.

"Could this be my door to a new path?" I whispered to the empty room. My fingertips grazed my ankles, traveled up the arches, and brushed across the toes. They were just feet—my feet—but through another's eyes, they could be art, a silent poetry of form and grace.

I reached for my phone, my hand trembling with a cocktail of fear and excitement. Each digit dialed was a step closer to the unknown. The ringtone was a siren song, seductive and alarming, pulling me toward a destiny not yet written.

"Hello?" The voice on the other end was crisp and professional.

"Hi, this is Jill Hills. I was given your number by Mr. Harold Johnson regarding... foot modeling." The words tasted strange on my tongue, an exotic flavor.

"Ah, yes, Jill! We've been expecting your call. Mr. Johnson speaks very highly of you. Let me see if he is available."

As I listened to the hold music, my heart danced a rhythm of possibility. With each passing moment, the layers of doubt shed away, revealing the budding confidence beneath. This was the turning point; I could feel it in the soles of my feet, the depth of my being. I was stepping into a world where my uniqueness was the key to an uncharted journey—a journey of self- discovery.

The call ended with a promise of things to come, a schedule for a photoshoot penciled into the near future. I lowered the phone, my heart still pounding within its cage of ribs. The silence around me felt heavy with potential, each second ticking by like a soft drumbeat heralding the start of a new chapter in my life.

I was alone, yet I felt the presence of countless possibilities fluttering around me like moths drawn to the warm glow of opportunity. My feet—once just an afterthought tucked into well- worn sneakers or hidden beneath the folds of blankets at night—were now stepping onto center stage, basking in a spotlight I never imagined could shine on me.

As the sun dipped below the horizon, casting long shadows across my room, a reflection caught my eye. There, in the mirror, stood a girl who was familiar and yet... transformed. Was this the same Jill Hills who had walked the halls of her high school with no grander ambition than to make it through another day unscathed? Or was she now someone sculpted by fate's insistent hands into a form not yet fully understood?

A smile tugged at the corners of my lips as I pondered the strange serendipity that had led Mr. Johnson to walk through the thrift store doors and into my life. His words had planted a seed of curiosity within me, one that had taken root and unfurled leaves of confidence with each passing day.

"I will pay you for them. And I pay well," he confidently told me.

"Feet," I mused aloud, dropping my gaze to my toes. They wiggled back at me as if acknowledging their part in this dance of destiny. I thought about the care I had started to lavish upon them, the lotions that scented my skin with lavender and vanilla, the careful trimming and shaping of nails that gleamed like pearls under the lamplight.

Could something as simple as feet carry me towards a bright future with promise? The idea was as daunting as it was thrilling, wrapping around my thoughts like silk ribbons, binding me to dreams I hadn't dared to dream.

"Jill Hills, foot model." The words felt foreign yet intoxicating, rolling off my tongue and filling the room with their whispered potential. I imagined cameras clicking, lights flashing, and eyes—all eyes—on the curves and lines that had, until now, only known the anonymity of everyday life.

Tonight, the world seemed to hold its breath along with me, waiting to exhale into whatever came next. I lay back on my bed, my feet propped up against the cool wall, as if presenting themselves to the universe. A small laugh escaped me, borne from a mixture of nerves and elation.

"Let's see where you can take me," I whispered to them, to myself, to the future that awaited just beyond the threshold of daring.

It started with Mr. Johnson taking sample pictures of my feet. Before long, I found myself attending his photo shoots, stepping into a world where my feet were the stars. With each successful gig with him, my confidence grew, and I marveled at how far I had come from that fateful summer day when an older man first complimented my feet.

As I delved deeper into the world of foot modeling, I discovered a hidden passion for the art of showcasing feet. Each photo shoot was like a dance, where my feet became the graceful performers under the spotlight. Not only were it my feet, but what my feet were in! The shoes, from stilettos to boots, platforms, stockings, and socks. The choices were endless, and Mr. Johnson paid for them all.

Discovering a Niche Market

As time went on, I noticed that there was a niche market for foot pictures. People were willing to pay good money for photos of well-maintained feet, even dirty feet. Intrigued by this opportunity, I decided to explore it further. I researched the industry, studied various foot modeling techniques, and even took professional photographs to see how my feet would fare in the market.

Late one evening, nestled among the soft throws on my bed, I opened my laptop and began scouring the internet for information on foot modeling. I delved into articles, forums, and portfolios, absorbing every detail of this niche market. It was a world where the arch of a foot, the grace of elongated toes, and the health of one's skin could become art and tell a story without uttering a single word.

I found an enormous market selling my feet pictures in the sexual foot fetish industry. My fingers danced over the keys as I connected with online communities, asking questions and seeking advice. The responses flooded in, friendly voices from around the globe sharing tips on posture, angles, and how to build a portfolio. A sensual mood enveloped me, one of anticipation and the intoxicating scent of opportunity.

"Could this be a part of who I am?" I wondered, my heart thrumming with each new discovery. The reflection in the mirror showed a young woman on the brink of self-discovery, her gaze alight with the embers of potential.

I jotted down notes, sketched poses, and even practiced positioning my feet under the soft glow of my desk lamp, imagining the camera's lens capturing their form. With every stretch and curl of my toes, I sensed a transformation unfurling within—a blossoming confidence that craved expression.

"Embrace your uniqueness, Jill," I whispered to myself, reaffirming the decision to explore this unconventional path. "Let your feet tell their own story."

The night stretched on, quiet save for the tapping of keys and the occasional sighs of contentment. It was a slow dance of research and reflection, one that promised to lead me to places I had only just begun to envision.

And there, bathed in the silver light of the moon filtering through my window, I felt the pull of a future rich with unknowns—a journey of beauty and self-expression waiting to be taken step by step.

The world of sexual foot fetishes is a realm of exquisite pleasure, where the sensual allure of the human foot takes center stage. In this erotic marketplace, I reveled in the admiration and desire men had for my feet, as their image became highly sought after by those with a penchant for this particular pleasure.

Some men would want a footjob. A footjob, as those in the know would call it, is an act of sexual gratification that involves the use of one's feet to stimulate a partner's genitals. The beauty of this act lies in its creativity, as there are countless ways to execute a footjob, each with its own unique sensation.

Imagine the scene: my feet, soft and supple, are adorned with delicate anklets that jingle softly with each movement. My partner lies before me, their eyes fixated on my every move as I slowly approach. I begin by running my toes lightly over their inner thighs, teasing them with the promise of what's to come. They tremble with anticipation, their breath hitching in their throat as I inch closer to their throbbing member.

Finally, I make contact, wrapping my feet around their shaft and beginning to stroke slowly. My super-high arches wrap around their cock. The feeling of their hard length sliding between my arches sends shivers down my spine, and I can't help but let out a low moan of pleasure. My partner responds in kind, their hips bucking up to meet my feet as I increase the pace.

The sensation of their smooth skin against my own is intoxicating, and I find myself lost in the rhythm of our movements. My feet work in tandem, gripping and releasing, twisting and sliding, as I bring my partner closer and closer to the edge.

But this is just the beginning. The world of foot fetishes is vast and varied, and there are so many erotic possibilities to explore. Perhaps it's the feeling of a partner's lips on your toes, or the tickling sensation of a feather tracing a path up your arch. Maybe it's the thrill of watching someone worship your feet, kissing and licking every inch of your sole.

Whatever the fantasy, the erotic potential of the human foot is undeniable. When I sold my pictures to the eager buyers in this sexual marketplace, I couldn't help but feel a sense of power and pride. For I know my feet can bring immense pleasure and satisfaction, and that there will always be a demand for this unique fetish.

Turning Passion into Profit

Turning my passion for foot fetish modeling into a profitable venture was an empowering journey. It allowed me to embrace my interests while connecting with a community that appreciated and valued this unique aspect of sexuality.

Many people may not understand the appeal of what I was doing (especially not my friends or my family). Still, there's something deeply intimate about feet—whether it's their beauty or the sensations they can evoke during activities like footjobs, foot massage, or tickling the feet. This connection opens doors to explore creativity and sensuality in ways I never imagined.

I discovered how many individuals were eager for this experience by sharing content that celebrated my feet. My work empowered them to express their desires without shame and brought pleasure into both our lives.

With platforms dedicated to adult content, monetization becomes feasible through subscriptions, tips, and custom requests. The financial rewards have allowed foot models more freedom in life while doing something they love.

Finding Balance and New Beginnings

As I dipped my toes into the world of foot modeling, pun intended, I found myself wading in a sea of pleasure and financial satisfaction. Men paid handsomely for the privilege of worshipping my feet. It started innocently enough, with foot massages and admiration, but as time went on, their desires became bolder. I gave my first-ever footjob, and the rest, as they say, is her story.

One client was a well-groomed executive, his suit expertly tailored to conceal his secret desires. His breath hitched as he unzipped his pants, revealing his hardness. "May I...?" he asked, his voice trembling. I nodded, and he gently placed his erection between my arches. With a delicate touch, I massaged him, alternating pressure and speed as I watched his face contort with pleasure.

It was surreal, witnessing the power my body, my feet held over him, the control I wielded with each stroke of my foot. He moaned, and I felt a thrill course through me, one I'd never experienced before.

Another client requested toe sucking, and I obliged, my stomach fluttering as his warm, wet mouth engulfed my toe digits. I'd never considered this an erogenous zone, but the sensation was indescribable. I found myself blushing as I felt a tingling sensation between my legs, a response I hadn't anticipated. My client's warm, wet mouth wrapped around my toes, causing an electrifying sensation to shoot up my legs. I couldn't help but let out a soft moan as I began to explore my own body. I slid my hand down my torso, tracing the curves of my hips before finally reaching the apex of my thighs. My fingers gently brushed against my clit, sending a jolt of pleasure through me. I was already soaking wet and couldn't wait to feel more.

I rubbed my clit in slow, circular motions, savoring every second of it. My breathing became heavier as I continued to pleasure myself, and I couldn't help but imagine what it would be like to have my client's tongue on my most sensitive spot. I slid two fingers inside myself, feeling the warmth and wetness that awaited me. I moved my fingers in and out, building up a steady rhythm that had me gasping for breath.

My client's mouth moved from my toes to my ankles, leaving a trail of wet kisses along the way. I could feel their hands exploring my legs, and I knew they were getting just as turned on as I was. I increased the speed of my fingers, feeling the familiar tingling sensation building up inside me. My muscles tensed, and I knew I was close. So close!

With one final thrust of my fingers, I let out a loud moan as waves of pleasure washed over me. My body convulsed, and I reveled in the feeling of release. I slowly dragged my fingers out, feeling completely satisfied. My client looked up at me with a satisfied smile, and I knew we had both enjoyed ourselves immensely.

In scientific detail, the stimulation of the clitoris sends signals to the brain that release dopamine, a feel-good chemical. The vagina also self-lubricates in response to arousal, allowing for smoother penetration. During orgasm, the muscles of the vagina and uterus contract, causing a rush of blood to the area and resulting in intense pleasure. The feet and toes are full of nerve endings. The stimulation of your feet can heighten the senses and make the sexual experience even more pleasurable.

Masturbation requests came next, and I admit I was hesitant at first. But the men were respectful, and their appreciation for my feet was almost reverential. I watched, transfixed, as they stroked themselves, eyes locked on my toes, and I couldn't help but feel flattered by their adoration.

As they climaxed, they groaned out their gratitude, and I couldn't help but feel a sense of accomplishment. I'd given them something they craved and couldn't find elsewhere, and they were willing to pay for it.

My bank account swelled, but more importantly, so did my self-confidence. I was no longer the shy, fumbling teenager I once was; I'd blossomed into a self-assured young woman, embracing my sexuality and unique talents.

Much to my surprise, my friends and most of my family eventually came around after I explained what I was doing and why. They were supportive, even intrigued, and while none of them were quite as adventurous as me, they understood my choices and accepted me for who I'd become.

Lunches and movie nights resumed, and my newfound experiences punctuated our conversations. They'd blush and giggle as I recounted my latest session, but underneath their teasing, I knew they were proud of me, of how far I'd come. I was doing something I liked, earning money and, most of all, being safe about it.

The foot modeling world opened my eyes to a new realm of pleasure and financial freedom. Still, more importantly, it had given me the confidence to embrace my body and my desires without shame or reservation. I'd discovered a newfound appreciation for my feet and their power over others. And for that, I will always be grateful for my unexpected detour into the world of foot fetish modeling.

Then I met him.

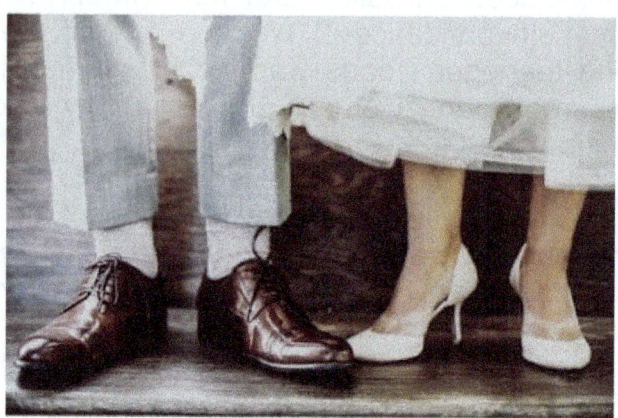

Foster was different from the other men I'd met on my journey. He was kind, soft-spoken, and breathtakingly handsome: yes, but it was his gentle demeanor and genuine interest in my well- being that captivated me. He saw past the polished exterior I'd created for myself and saw the woman beneath, the girl who'd once blushed at the thought of baring her soles to a stranger.

Slowly, hesitantly, we began to date. Afternoon coffee dates turned into romantic dinners, and before I knew it, we were inseparable.

Foster didn't judge me for my unconventional past or ask me to change. He accepted me for who I was, calluses and all.

One warm summer evening, as we strolled barefoot along the beach, he knelt in the sand and proposed with a ring that glittered as brightly as my newly manicured nails. Tears of happiness spilled down my cheeks as I said yes, not just to him, but to a new life.

The wedding was small and intimate, attended by a handful of close friends and family. I wore a simple white gown that ended just above my ankles, showcasing my perfect pedicure and bearing witness to the road I'd traveled to get where I was now.

As we danced our first dance, the familiar strains of *Stand By Me* by Ben E. King played in the background; I looked into my new husband's eyes and knew I'd found my true calling.

At that moment, I realized that my foot fetish modeling career had shaped me, but it no longer defined me. I'd found my own version of happily ever after, and my soles have never been more at peace.

Chapter Three

Setting Up Your Feet Picture Business

Creating a Professional Online Presence

Creating a professional online presence is crucial for anyone looking to succeed in the business of selling feet pictures online. It is essential to showcase your feet in the best possible light to attract potential buyers. This subchapter will provide valuable insights and strategies for establishing a strong and professional online presence that will set you apart from the competition.

The first step in creating a professional online presence is establishing a strong brand identity. This includes creating a unique brand that reflects your personal style and developing a consistent tone of voice (type of images) for your online content. Creating a cohesive brand image will make it easier for potential buyers to recognize and remember your feet pictures.

In addition to branding, optimizing your online platforms for selling feet pictures is essential. This includes setting up a user-friendly website or social media profiles where customers can easily browse and purchase your images. It is also necessary to regularly update your content and engage with your audience to build trust and credibility.

Marketing strategies are crucial in promoting your feet pictures and attracting potential buyers. Utilize social media platforms, email marketing, and online advertising to reach a wider audience and drive traffic to your online platforms. You can increase your visibility and boost your sales by implementing effective marketing strategies.

Lastly, remember to consider legal aspects when selling feet pictures online. Familiarize yourself with copyright laws, privacy policies, and other legal considerations to protect yourself and your business. You may want to consider consulting with an attorney. Following these guidelines and creating a professional online presence can establish a successful feet picture business and make you stand out in the competitive market.

Setting Prices for Your Feet Pictures

Setting prices for your feet pictures is an important aspect of running a successful business in this niche market. As a female foot model or aspiring entrepreneur in the feet picture industry, it is crucial to understand the value of your work and how to price it accordingly. There are several factors to consider when determining the price of your feet pictures, including the quality of the images, the demand for your content, and the platform on which you are selling.

One key factor to consider when setting prices for your feet pictures is the quality of the images. High-quality, well-lit, well-composed, and visually appealing photos will typically command higher prices than lower-quality images. Investing in professional photography equipment or hiring a photographer can help you create stunning images to attract more buyers and justify a higher price point for your work. However, you do not need to hire a professional photographer and spend money on the latest equipment to get started. Many phone cameras are more than capable of creating stunning images. Affordable light equipment can be found on Amazon.

Another important consideration when pricing your feet pictures is the demand for your content. If you have a large social media following or a dedicated fan base willing to pay a premium for your photos, you can afford to charge higher prices for your work. On the other hand, if you are starting in the industry and are looking to build your brand, you may need to price your pictures lower initially to attract customers and generate interest in your work.

The platform on which you are selling your feet pictures can also impact your chosen pricing strategy. Some platforms may have restrictions on pricing or may take a commission from each sale, so it is important to research the terms and conditions of different platforms before setting your prices. Additionally, some platforms cater to a specific niche market or demographic, so you may need to adjust your prices to appeal to the target audience of each platform.

In conclusion, setting prices for your feet pictures is a nuanced process that requires careful consideration of multiple factors. By focusing on the quality of your images, the demand for your content, and the platform you are selling, you can create a pricing strategy that maximizes your profits and attracts customers to your business. Remember to regularly reassess your pricing strategy based on market trends and customer feedback to ensure continued success in the feet picture industry.

Building a Portfolio of Feet Pictures

Building a portfolio of foot pictures is essential in establishing a successful business selling foot pictures online. As a female foot model looking to capitalize on this growing market, it is crucial to curate a collection of high-quality images that showcase your feet in the best possible light. Your portfolio should reflect various styles, poses, and angles to appeal to a wide range of potential customers.

When building your portfolio, pay attention to the details. Take the time to ensure that your feet are well-groomed and manicured, as this will enhance the overall quality of your pictures.
Experiment with different lighting techniques and backgrounds to create visually appealing images that stand out from the competition. Consider enlisting the help or advice of a photographer to capture stunning shots that highlight the beauty of your feet. Also, you can read many internet articles about building a

model portfolio.

In addition to the aesthetic aspects of your portfolio, it is also crucial to consider the marketing strategies that will help you sell your feet pictures online. Use social media platforms like Instagram and Twitter to showcase your portfolio and attract potential customers. Engage with your followers by posting regularly and promptly responding to comments and inquiries. Collaborate with other influencers in the feet picture industry to expand your reach and attract new clients.

When selecting platforms for selling your feet pictures, consider your target audience's specific needs and preferences. Choose platforms offering secure payment options and a user-friendly interface for buyers and sellers—research different websites and apps to find the best fit for your business model and marketing strategy. Be sure to read the terms and conditions of each platform carefully to ensure that you comply with all legal considerations related to selling feet pictures online.

As you continue to build your brand and establish yourself in the feet picture market, focus on creating a unique and recognizable style that sets you apart from the competition. Develop a signature look for your feet pictures that resonates with your target audience and reinforces your brand identity. You can use editing software to produce professional-looking images at a premium price. By building a solid portfolio of feet pictures and implementing effective marketing strategies, you can set yourself up for success in the lucrative world of selling feet pictures online.

Chapter Four

Marketing Strategies for Selling Feet Pictures Online

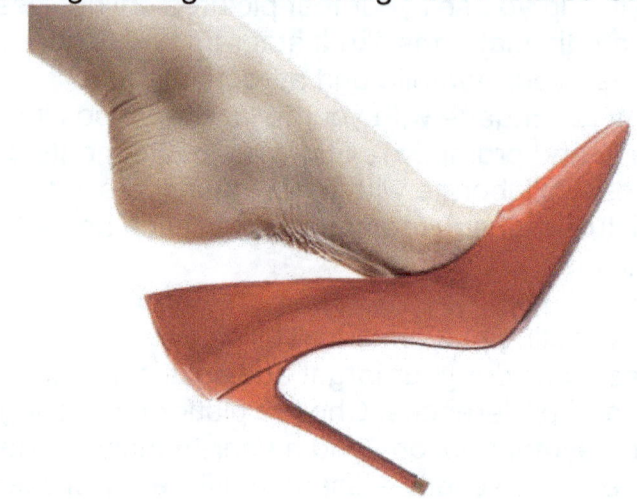

Social media has become an essential tool for promoting and selling products and services in the digital age. It can be a game-changer for female foot models looking to capitalize on the lucrative market for foot pictures. By leveraging platforms such as Instagram, Twitter, and TikTok, women can reach a broad audience of potential buyers and build a successful foot- picture business from the ground up.

You are setting up a successful business when selling feet pictures online, which requires more than just taking attractive photos. Developing a marketing strategy that effectively promotes your brand and drives sales is essential. Social media platforms offer a unique opportunity to engage with customers, showcase your products, and build a loyal following.

By creating compelling content that highlights the beauty and uniqueness of your feet, you can attract a dedicated fan base and increase your chances of making sales.

One of the key benefits of using social media to promote your feet pictures is the ability to target specific demographics and niches. Using hashtags, geotags, and other targeting tools, you can reach individuals interested in purchasing feet pictures and willing to pay a premium for high-quality content. Additionally, social media platforms offer a range of advertising options that can help you reach a larger audience and drive more traffic to your online store. Just ensure you follow their terms of service so your account is not flagged.

In addition to marketing your feet pictures on social media, it's essential to consider the legal considerations of selling this type of content online. Be sure to familiarize yourself with the laws and regulations surrounding the sale of adult content and take steps to protect your intellectual property. By staying informed and compliant with legal guidelines, you can avoid potential legal issues and ensure a smooth and successful business operation.

Utilizing social media to promote your feet pictures can be a powerful tool for female foot models looking to build a successful business in this niche market. By developing a solid marketing strategy, targeting specific demographics, and staying informed about legal considerations, you can create a thriving brand that attracts loyal customers and generates consistent sales. With the right approach and dedication, selling feet pictures online can be a lucrative and rewarding venture for women looking to monetize their unique assets.

In selling feet pictures online, collaborating with influencers can be another game-changer for your business. Influencers have the power to reach a large audience and can help you gain exposure and credibility in the industry. By partnering with influencers in the feet picture industry, you can tap into their loyal following and expand your reach to potential customers interested in purchasing your high-quality feet pictures.

When collaborating with influencers, it is important to choose individuals who align with your brand and target audience. Look for influencers who have a strong presence in the feet picture niche and who have a large following. By partnering with influencers in your target market, you can ensure that your feet pictures will be promoted to the right audience and have a higher chance of converting into sales.

To successfully collaborate with influencers in the feet picture industry, it's essential to establish clear expectations and goals for the partnership. Discuss the terms of the collaboration, including compensation, promotion schedule, and deliverables. Ensure you communicate your brand message and key selling points so the influencer can effectively promote your feet pictures to their audience authentically and engagingly.

In addition to collaborating with influencers, consider leveraging their platforms to host giveaways, contests, or exclusive promotions for your feet pictures. This can generate buzz around your brand and attract new customers to your online store. Offering special deals or discounts through influencer partnerships can incentivize potential buyers to purchase and increase your sales revenue.

Collaborating with influencers in the feet picture industry can be a valuable strategy for building brand awareness, expanding your reach, and driving sales for your online business.

Running Promotions and Sales to Attract Customers

Running promotions and sales can be a great way to attract customers to your feet picture business. By offering discounts, special deals, or limited-time offers, you can entice potential buyers to purchase. One effective strategy is to provide a discount for first-time customers or a buy-one-get-one-free deal to encourage repeat business. You can also create themed sales events around holidays or special occasions to generate excitement and drive sales. Put little Santa hats on each toe, or paint your toenails green for St. Patrick's Day.

When running promotions and sales, it's important to promote them effectively to reach your target audience. Utilize social media platforms, email marketing, and online advertising to spread the word about your special offers. Consider partnering with influencers or bloggers in the feet picture niche to help promote your sales to a broader audience. Creating a buzz around your promotions can attract more customers and increase your sales.

In addition to offering discounts and special deals, consider running contests or giveaways to engage your audience and attract new customers. Encourage participants to share your promotions on social media or sign up for your email list to enter the contest. This can help increase brand visibility and grow your customer base. You can also offer exclusive access to limited-edition feet pictures or behind-the-scenes content to incentivize participation in your promotions.

You can keep your audience engaged and returning for more by running promotions and sales regularly. Monitor the performance of your promotions to see what resonates with your customers and adjust your strategy accordingly. By experimenting with different offers and incentives, you can find what works best for your feet picture business and continue to attract new customers. Remember to stay consistent with your promotional efforts to maintain a steady sales flow and grow your business over time.

In conclusion, running promotions and sales is a crucial strategy for attracting customers to your feet picture business. You can incentivize purchases and engage your audience by offering discounts, special deals, contests, and giveaways. Promote your promotions effectively through social media, email marketing, and influencer partnerships to reach a wider audience. Monitor the performance of your promotions and adjust your strategy as needed to maximize sales and grow your business. A well-executed promotional plan can attract more customers and establish a successful feet picture business.

Chapter Five

Platforms for Selling Feet Pictures

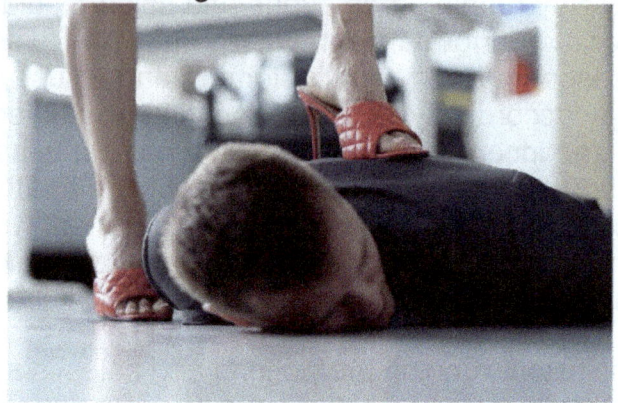

In today's digital age, selling feet pictures online has become a popular way for women, especially female models, to earn extra income. Several websites cater to this niche market, offering a platform for individuals to showcase and sell their feet pictures to interested buyers. These websites provide a convenient and discreet way for women to monetize their unique assets without face-to-face interactions.

One of the most popular websites for selling pictures of feet is OnlyFans. This platform allows creators to set up a profile, upload photos and videos, and set prices for their content. OnlyFans has gained a reputation for its user-friendly interface and high level of security, making it a preferred choice for many women looking to sell foot pictures online. Creators can also interact with their fans through direct messages and live streams, creating a more personalized buyer experience.

Two other popular websites for selling pictures of feet are FeetFinder and FunwithFeet. These platforms specifically cater to the foot fetish community, providing a targeted audience for women looking to sell their feet pictures. They offer various features, such as customizable profiles, messaging options, and payment processing, making it easy for creators to connect with potential buyers and make sales. With its focus on foot-related content, FeetFinder and FunwithFeet are an excellent option for women who want to target a specific niche market and make money.

When setting up a successful feet picture business, it is essential to consider marketing strategies that will help attract buyers and generate sales. Social media platforms like Instagram, Twitter, and TikTok can help creators reach a wider audience and drive traffic to their selling platforms. By posting high-quality photos and engaging with followers, women can build a strong brand presence and establish themselves as reputable sellers in the feet picture industry.

Legal considerations are also important when selling feet pictures online. Creators should know copyright laws, privacy regulations, and age restrictions to ensure they comply with all legal requirements. Photos should be watermarked to protect intellectual property and verify buyers' age to prevent potential legal issues.

By staying informed and following best practices, women can run a successful feet picture business while staying within legal boundaries.

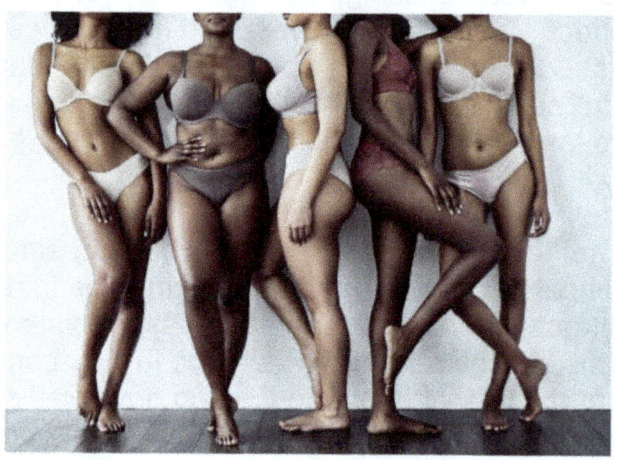

Choosing the right platform for your feet picture business is crucial in ensuring the success of your venture. With so many options available, it can be overwhelming to decide where to start. As a female model looking to sell feet pictures online, you want to reach the right audience and maximize your profits. This subchapter will explore the various platforms and help you determine the best fit for your business.

When choosing a platform for your feet picture business, consider your target audience and the features offered by each platform. Some platforms cater specifically to the foot fetish community, while others have a broader audience. Choosing a platform that aligns with your brand and values is essential. Additionally, look for platforms that offer user-friendly interfaces, secure payment options, and strong customer support.

As mentioned above, OnlyFans, FunwithFeet, and Feetfinder are popular platforms for selling foot pictures online. These platforms allow creators to monetize their content through subscriptions and tips, an excellent option for building a loyal fan base and generating a steady income. Another platform to consider is Patreon, which allows creators to offer exclusive content to their subscribers. Patreon is ideal for building a community around your feet picture business and engaging with your fans more personally. Another platform worthy of mentioning is Feetify. Feetify promotes the idea of interaction between customers and sellers. This website is popular because it creates a marketplace where people can engage and make successful sales. This platform gives sellers the means to interact and conduct business successfully in the foot- picture niche while encapsulating the essence of a close-knit community.

If you prefer a more traditional e-commerce platform, consider setting up a website using Wix, WordPress, or Squarespace. These platforms offer customizable templates and easy-to-use tools for creating a professional online store. You can showcase your feet pictures, set your prices, and manage orders in one place. With the right marketing strategies, you can drive traffic to your website and increase sales.

In conclusion, choosing the right platform for your

feet picture business is critical in building a successful online venture. Consider your target audience, features offered, and branding when deciding which platform to use. Whether you choose OnlyFans, Patreon, Feetfinder, Feetify, or your own website, focus on creating high-quality feet pictures, marketing your business effectively, and building a solid brand presence. You can turn your passion for feet photos into a profitable business with the right platform and strategies.

Setting Up Shop on Multiple Platforms for Maximum Exposure

In the world of selling feet pictures online, it's important to maximize your exposure to reach a larger audience and increase your chances of making sales. One way to do this is by setting up shop on multiple platforms. By diversifying where you sell your photos, you can attract different types of buyers and increase your visibility in the market.

When choosing which platforms to sell on, you must consider where your target audience is most likely to be. For example, platforms like Instagram and TikTok may be more effective if you're targeting a younger demographic. On the other hand, if you want to reach a more mature audience, sites like OnlyFans, Feetify, or FeetFinder may better suit your needs.

You can also use each platform's unique features and tools by setting up shop on multiple platforms. For example, some platforms may offer built-in marketing tools or analytics to help you track your progress and make informed decisions about your business. Utilizing these tools across multiple platforms allows you to optimize your marketing strategies and maximize your chances of success.

Another benefit of selling on multiple platforms is that it can help you establish your brand and build credibility in the industry. By being present on several different platforms, you can show potential buyers that you are a serious and professional seller who is dedicated to providing high-quality content. This can help you stand out from the competition and attract more customers to your business.

However, it's important to remember that each platform has rules and regulations for selling adult content, including foot pictures. Before setting up shop on multiple platforms, familiarize yourself with each platform's terms of service and ensure that you comply with all legal considerations. By following the rules and guidelines set forth by each platform, you can protect yourself from potential legal issues and establish a reputable business within the industry.

Chapter Six

Legal Considerations for Selling Feet Pictures

Understanding Copyright Laws for Feet Pictures

Understanding copyright laws is crucial for selling foot pictures online. Knowing your rights and responsibilities as a content creator is vital as a female foot model looking to capitalize on this niche market. Copyright laws protect your original work from being used or reproduced without your permission. This includes photos of the feet that you are looking to sell.

When you take a photograph of your feet, you automatically own the copyright to that image. This means you have the exclusive rights to reproduce, distribute, and display that image. However, it is important to note that copyright laws can vary by country, so it is essential to familiarize yourself with the laws in your jurisdiction. By understanding copyright laws, you can protect your intellectual property and prevent others from using your feet pictures without your consent.

One important aspect of copyright laws to consider is licensing. When you sell your feet pictures online, you essentially license the use of your images to others. Clearly outlining the terms of this license is crucial, including specifying how the photos can be used, where they can be displayed, and for how long. By setting clear guidelines for using your feet pictures, you can protect your rights and prevent any potential misuse of your images.

In addition to licensing, it is crucial to consider the potential for infringement when selling feet pictures online. Unfortunately, some individuals may try to use your images without your permission, damaging your brand and reputation. Understanding copyright laws and taking steps to protect your images can minimize the risk of infringement and ensure that your pictures are used legally and ethically.

Understanding copyright laws is essential for any female foot model looking to sell foot pictures online. By knowing your rights, licensing your images correctly, and protecting your intellectual property, you can build a successful feet picture business while safeguarding your work from unauthorized use. With a solid understanding of copyright laws, you can confidently market and sell your high-quality feet pictures on various platforms, all while building a solid and reputable brand in this niche market.

Ensuring Privacy and Safety for Yourself and Your Customers

When selling pictures of feet online, ensuring privacy and safety for yourself and your customers is paramount. As a female entrepreneur in this niche market, it is crucial to take the necessary steps to protect both your personal information and your clients. By implementing the right strategies and practices, you can create a safe and secure environment for conducting business and building your brand.

Establishing clear boundaries with your customers is one of the first steps in ensuring privacy and safety. Communicate your expectations for behavior and make it known that any form of harassment or inappropriate conduct will not be tolerated. By setting these boundaries from the beginning, you can create a safer space for yourself and your clients to engage in transactions and interactions.

Another critical aspect of protecting privacy and safety is using secure platforms for selling foot pictures. Choose reputable websites and platforms with robust security measures to protect your data and that of your customers. By conducting transactions on secure platforms, you can minimize the risk of data breaches and ensure that sensitive information remains confidential.

When marketing your feet pictures online, be mindful

of the information you share and how you present yourself. Avoid revealing personal details that could compromise your safety, such as your real full or partial name, address, or personal contact information. Instead, focus on creating a professional and enticing brand image that showcases your pictures tastefully and appealingly.

Lastly, consider investing in legal protections to safeguard your business and intellectual property. Consult with a lawyer to draft terms of service agreements, privacy policies, and copyright protections that outline your rights and responsibilities as a feet picture seller. These proactive steps can protect yourself and your customers while building a successful and sustainable business in the online feet picture market.

Dealing with Potential Legal Issues in the Feet Picture Industry

Awareness of potential legal issues is essential when selling feet pictures online. As a female model looking to enter the feet picture industry, protecting yourself and your business from legal troubles is crucial. In this subchapter, we will discuss some common legal considerations you should consider as you navigate the world of selling feet pictures.

One of the leading legal issues that can arise in the feet picture industry is copyright infringement. It's essential to ensure you have the right to use any images or content you include in your feet pictures. If you are using images belonging to someone else, you could be at risk of legal action for copyright infringement. Make sure to use only images you have the right to or that are in the public domain to avoid potential legal issues.

Another legal consideration when selling pictures of feet is the issue of consent. It's essential to ensure that you have permission from any individuals whose feet are featured in your photographs. Without proper consent, you could risk facing legal action for invasion of privacy or similar charges. Always obtain written permission from any individuals whose feet you plan to photograph and sell pictures of.

Additionally, knowing any laws or regulations that may apply to selling foot pictures in your area is important. Some jurisdictions may have specific laws regarding the sale of adult content or images of feet. Familiarize yourself with relevant laws and regulations to ensure that you operate within the law's bounds.

It's a good idea to consult a legal professional specializing in this area to protect yourself from potential legal issues. They can help you navigate the legal landscape of selling feet pictures and ensure you comply with all relevant laws and regulations. By proactively addressing potential legal issues, you can protect yourself and your business from any legal troubles that may arise.

Short-Form General Photography Contract

This agreement is between PHOTOGRAPHER NAME or COMPANY Photography (hereafter "Photographer" "the Photographer" or "Photography Company") and _____ (hereafter referred to as "CLIENT").

Scope of Work:

This contract is for services and products related to a photography shoot (hereafter "shoot" or "the shoot") to take place at the following time and place.

PHOTOGRAPHER and CLIENT are to arrive for the SHOOT at _____(time) at _____(place).

PHOTOGRAPHER agrees to provide at least ____ photos for CLIENT to view after the shoot and is not required to provide more than this number of images. PHOTOGRAPHER will perform basic post-processing or digital image editing services on these photos where artistically necessary.

In consideration for the photography services provided by PHOTOGRAPHER, CLIENT agrees to pay the sum of _____. CLIENT agrees to pay the photographer a non-refundable initial payment of _ towards this sum, upon signing this contract. The initial payment reserved the photographer's time and is not a retainer or deposit. PHOTOGRAPHER agrees not to advertise the availability of this same time slot to any other potential clients. If CLIENT cancels this shoot, the initial payment will not be returned to CLIENT.

The balance of the payment for photography services must be paid in full no later than seven (7) days after the SHOOT detailed in Section 1: Scope of Work. Photo proofs will not be provided until CLIENT has paid in full. If CLIENT is required to purchase photos separately after the SHOOT, payment for those photos is due immediately upon delivery of photos to CLIENT.

Work Product

The PHOTOGRAPHER will deliver proofs to the CLIENT within thirty days (30) after the SHOOT date. The CLIENT understands and agrees that the proofs are the exclusive property of the PHOTOGRAPHER and that the CLIENT has no right to these photos except for a license to review them but not store them.

All photos delivered to CLIENT are licensed for CLIENT'S personal use only. Any images from the SHOOT posted on social media must be credited to the PHOTOGRAPHER. Pictures from the SHOOT to be delivered to the CLIENT will follow this order.

Are any photos to be included in the price for photography services? YES or NO, ALL PHOTOS MUST BE PURCHASED SEPARATELY

How many photos -- included in the price – will be licensed to CLIENT, and in what resolution?

How many prints – included in the price – will be delivered to CLIENT, in what sizes, and what materials will be used for printing?

CLIENT understands and agrees that prints take longer to deliver. PHOTOGRAPHER must deliver the photos within 45 days after the CLIENT has made a final order.

Indemnification:

    1. – PHOTOGRAPHER and CLIENT agree that PHOTOGRAPHER is not obligated to capture any specific moment, pose, or person(s) during the SHOOT.

    2. – If PHOTOGRAPHER is unable to perform the services in this contract due to any cause outside its control, CLIENT agrees to indemnify PHOTOGRAPHER for any loss, damage, or liability; however, PHOTOGRAPHER will return in full all payments made by CLIENT to PHOTOGRAPHER concerning this SHOOT.

3. – CLIENT agrees to indemnify and hold harmless PHOTOGRAPHER for any liability, damage, or loss related to technological failure, including data loss.

4. – CLIENT understands and agrees that PHOTOGRAPHER is not required to maintain copies of the photos from this SHOOT sixty (60) days after the images have been delivered to CLIENT.

5. – CLIENT agrees to hold PHOTOGRAPHER harmless for any personal injury that may occur as the CLIENT poses or works with PHOTOGRAPHER.

6. – PHOTOGRAPHER will strive to present photos in a workmanlike manner but is not required to cater to the specific aesthetic preferences of the CLIENT.

Duty of Client

CLIENT will obtain all permissions necessary for PHOTOGRAPHER to photograph at the SHOOT. PHOTOGRAPHER has no duty to obtain permission from reception centers, churches, buildings, properties, or other locations to operate thereon. CLIENT understands and agrees that any failure to obtain these permissions resulting in fines to PHOTOGRAPHER, or which prevent PHOTOGRAPHER from photographing the event(s) is not the fault, liability, or responsibility of PHOTOGRAPHER.

Exclusive Photographer

CLIENT agrees and understands that no party other than the PHOTOGRAPHER may take photos of any poses, lighting situations, or setups made by the photographer. This slows down the photographer's work and violates the photographer's right to take photos of the event.
CLIENT agrees to take responsibility for insisting that no person(s) get in the way of the PHOTOGRAPHER or take pictures in these situations.

Model Release

CLIENT grants permission to PHOTOGRAPHER and its assignees, licensees, and sublicensees, permission to use CLIENT'S image or likeness in any and all forms of media for commercial purposes, advertising, trade, personal use, or any and all other uses. Therefore, PHOTOGRAPHER may use CLIENT'S likeness and image on PHOTOGRAPHER'S website or any other advertising.

Assignability and Parties of Interest

CLIENT agrees and understands that, unless

otherwise specified in this Contract, CLIENT is not contracting for personal services that any specific photographer will perform. PHOTOGRAPHER may sub-contract or assign this contract to any second-shooter. PHOTOGRAPHER may assign any photographers associated with the PHOTOGRAPHY COMPANY to perform its duties under this contract. All photographers must be capable and competent to perform the services in a workmanlike manner consistent with the aesthetic standards of the PHOTOGRAPHER.

PHOTOGRAPHER Signature _____
_____Date: _____

CLIENT Signature _____
_____Date: _____

Adult Model Release Agreement

The parties to this release agreement are:

Physical Address: _____
_____

Telephone Number and Email Address: _____
_____

(Hereinafter referred to as "the Model")

AND

Physical Address: _____
_____

Telephone Number and Email Address: _____
_____

(Hereinafter referred to as "the Photographer")

Whereas for valuable consideration hereby acknowledged as received, the Model granted the Photographer permission to photograph and/or film and sound record the Model and grant permission to use the resulting work ("the Work") according to the terms stated hereunder:

1. Any permission granted to the Photographer shall extend to his/her successors, legal representatives, licensees, and assigns and shall be irrevocable and perpetual without any further or additional claim for compensation by the Model.

1. Use of the Work shall be unrestricted as to

location, quantity or frequency, may be for any purpose and in any medium whatsoever, whether foreseen or unforeseen at this time, except where such use is in contravention of the law.

1. Permission is expressly granted for the Work to be edited, altered, distorted, used in whole or in part, in conjunction with other images, graphics, text, and sound in any way whatsoever and without restrictions.

1. Permission herein granted is absolute and final and shall not be subject to further inspection or approval by the Model at any stage in using the Work.

1. Use of the Work may be in conjunction with the Model's own or fictitious names.

1. The Photographer shall own all rights in the Work, which shall accrue to the benefit of his/her successors, legal representatives, and assigns.

1. Notwithstanding the above, the following uses are expressly noted and agreed to, and specific listed here shall take precedence and restrict the use of the Work accordingly:

_____

1. The Model warrants having read and understood this Model Release Agreement and warrants being of full legal age to agree.

1. With full knowledge of the above, the Model hereby releases and shall hold harmless the Photographer and his/her successors, legal representatives, licensees, and assigns from all claims or damages, including but not limited to defamation or violation of the right of privacy or publicity, resulting from or associated with the use of the Work.

1. The Model agrees that the provisions contained herein shall be binding upon the Model and his/her successors, legal representatives, and assigns.

1. This Agreement shall be construed, interpreted, and governed by the laws of the State of

_____, and should any provision of this Agreement be judged by an appropriate court as invalid, it shall not affect any of the remaining provisions whatsoever.

1. The parties agree that any or all parts of this agreement may be submitted to the other party in legible and recordable electronic form and, upon acknowledgment of receipt by the receiving party, shall become valid parts of the agreement.

Signed at _____ on this _____ day of
_____ 20_____

Model's Signature: _____
_____

Signed at _____ on this _____ day of
_____ 20_____

Photographer's Signature: _____
_____

In paragraph 7. of the above model release form, we provide space where sensitive issues can be addressed, specific locations/countries can be excluded, or uses may be excluded. For example, a Model may stipulate that their image may never be used in conjunction with crime, alcohol, drugs, or pornography websites. Similarly, if the Photographer intends to use the image in a campaign against women's abuse (or other sensitive issues), for example, that should be noted too. Both Photographer and Model must initial where any additions or alterations are made by hand.

Attach a sheet with thumbnails to the relevant model release form for your record keeping. You (the photographer) should also make a copy of the Model's identification document as proof of age and attach it to your photo release.

Chapter Seven

Building a Brand for Selling Feet Pictures

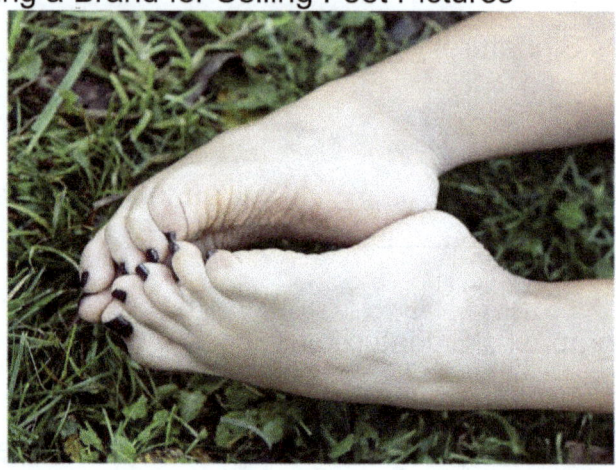

In the world of selling foot pictures online, setting yourself apart from the competition is crucial to developing a unique selling proposition (USP) that will attract potential buyers and keep them coming back for more. Your USP differentiates your feet pictures from others on the market and gives customers a reason to choose yours over someone else's. This could be anything from your photography style to the quality of your pictures or the specific niche you cater to.

When developing your USP, consider what sets your feet pictures apart from others. Are you someone with stunning feet who is in high demand? Do you have a specific collection of high heels that highlight your feet? Can you do things with your toes? Do you have a unique theme or style that sets your pictures apart? Whatever it is, ensure it resonates with your target audience and makes them want to buy from you.

Once you have identified your USP, make sure to highlight it in all of your marketing materials. Use it as a selling point in your product descriptions, social media posts, and website content. This will help customers understand what makes your feet pictures unique and why they should choose you over other sellers.

In addition to highlighting your USP, consistently deliver on your promises. If you claim to have the highest-quality pictures of feet, ensure your images are always top-notch. This will help you attract new customers and retain existing ones who trust you to deliver a superior product.

By developing a strong USP and consistently delivering on it, you can set yourself up for success in the competitive world of selling feet pictures online. Remember always to keep your target audience in mind and cater to their specific needs and desires. With a suitable USP, you can build a successful feet picture business that stands out and attracts loyal customers.

Creating a Memorable Brand Identity

Creating a memorable brand identity is crucial for selling foot pictures online. As a female foot model looking to break into the feet picture business, it's essential to establish a unique and recognizable brand that sets you apart from the competition. Your brand identity should reflect your personality, values, and aesthetics, helping to attract a loyal customer base and drive sales.

Consider your target audience, niche market, and competitive landscape when creating your brand identity. Consider what makes your feet pictures stand out and how to communicate that to potential customers. Choose a name, logo, color scheme, and overall aesthetic that align with your brand values and appeal to your target audience. Creating a cohesive and consistent brand identity can build customer trust and establish yourself as a reputable seller in the feet picture industry.

By building a solid brand identity, implementing effective marketing strategies, choosing the right platforms, and addressing legal considerations, you can create a successful feet picture business that stands out in the competitive online market.

Engaging with Your Audience to Build Brand Loyalty

Engaging with your audience is crucial for building brand loyalty when selling foot pictures online. As a female foot model or woman looking to profit from your feet, it's essential to establish a strong connection with your followers and potential customers. By engaging with your audience meaningfully, you can create a loyal fanbase that will keep returning for more of your high-quality feet pictures.

One way to engage with your audience is to interact with them on social media platforms. Respond to comments and messages, ask for feedback on your content, and create polls or surveys to get to know your audience better. Send birthday and holiday wishes or offer your discounts on those special days. By showing that you care about their opinions and input, you can build a sense of community around your brand and establish a loyal following of customers who appreciate your work.

Another effective way to engage with your audience is to offer exclusive content or behind-the- scenes access to your feet picture business. By giving your followers a glimpse into your creative process and the effort you put into creating high-quality feet pictures, you can build trust and loyalty with them. Consider offering special discounts or promotions to your most loyal customers to show appreciation for their support.

In addition to social media engagement, consider selling your used shoes or socks. This can be a great way to connect with your followers personally and build relationships beyond just buying and selling feet pictures. By creating a sense of community and belonging, you can turn casual followers into loyal customers who will continue to support your brand for years to come.

Engaging with your audience is a key strategy for building brand loyalty in the competitive world of selling feet pictures online. By interacting with your followers on social media, offering exclusive content, and selling physical items, you can create a solid and loyal fanbase to support your business long-term. Remember always to prioritize your customers' needs and preferences, and you'll be well on your way to building a successful feet picture business that stands out in the market.

Chapter Eight

Creating High-Quality Feet Pictures for Sale

As a female foot model looking to expand your income, selling foot pictures online can be lucrative. However, it's important to understand the art of taking professional foot pictures to succeed in this industry. Here are some tips to help you master the craft and attract potential buyers.

First and foremost, invest in a good-quality camera or smartphone with high-resolution capabilities. Clear, sharp images are essential in showcasing the details of your feet and enticing customers to make a purchase. Experiment with different angles, lighting, and backgrounds to find the most flattering and aesthetically pleasing shots.

When setting up your feet picture business, it's crucial to establish a strong brand identity. Choose a catchy, memorable name and create a cohesive theme for your images. Consistency in style and presentation will help you stand out in a crowded market and attract a loyal customer base.

Regarding marketing strategies, utilize social media platforms such as Instagram, Twitter, and TikTok to promote your feet pictures. Engage with your followers, post regularly, and use relevant hashtags to increase your visibility and reach a wider audience. Consider collaborating with other foot models or influencers to cross-promote each other's content and gain more exposure.

When choosing the right platform for selling your feet pictures, consider websites such as *OnlyFans*, *Patreon*, or *FeetFinder*. Research each platform's terms and conditions, payment options, and commission rates to determine which one aligns best with your business goals. Remember to also familiarize yourself with legal considerations, such as age restrictions and copyright laws, to protect yourself and your content.

Lastly, focus on creating high-quality, eye-catching foot pictures that showcase your unique style and personality. Experiment with different props, poses, and nail art to keep your content fresh and engaging. By following these tips and staying dedicated to your craft, you can build a successful foot picture business and establish yourself as a sought-after foot model in the online marketplace.

Editing and Enhancing Your Feet Pictures

Editing and enhancing your feet pictures is essential in creating high-quality images to attract potential buyers and help you stand out in a competitive market. In this subchapter, we will discuss some tips and techniques for editing and enhancing your feet pictures to make them more appealing to your target audience.

The first step in editing your feet pictures is to choose

the right editing software. Many options are available, from free online editors to more advanced programs like Adobe Photoshop, Lightroom, or Photo Director by Cyberlink. Experiment with different tools and features to find the ones that work best for you and your style.

Once you have chosen your editing software, the next step is to familiarize yourself with the basic editing techniques. This may include adjusting the brightness and contrast, cropping the image, and removing imperfections or distractions. Remember to focus on your feet and avoid over-editing, which can make your pictures look unnatural.

Enhancing your feet pictures can also involve adding filters, textures, or overlays to give them a unique and eye-catching look. Experiment with different effects to find the ones that complement your style and appeal to your target audience. Remember to stay true to your brand and aesthetic while editing your pictures.

Lastly, don't forget to optimize your images for online platforms by resizing them to the appropriate dimensions and file sizes. This will help your pictures load quickly and look their best on various devices. By editing and enhancing your feet pictures, you can create a cohesive and professional brand that will attract buyers and help you succeed in selling feet pictures online.

Keeping Up with Trends in Feet Picture Aesthetics

In the fast-paced world of online business, it's crucial to stay ahead of the curve when it comes to trends in feet picture aesthetics. As a female foot model looking to sell feet pictures online, it's essential to understand what styles and techniques are currently popular to attract a wider audience and increase your sales.

One key trend in feet picture aesthetics is using natural lighting to highlight the curves and details of the foot. By taking photos in natural light, you can create a more realistic and flattering image that will appeal to potential buyers. Additionally, experimenting with different angles and poses can help you showcase your feet in the most attractive way possible.

Another important aspect of keeping up with trends in feet picture aesthetics is staying current with popular editing techniques. Enhancing your photos with filters, effects, and touch-ups can help you create a more polished and professional look that will catch the eye of potential customers.

When setting up a successful feet picture business, you must understand marketing strategies that will help you reach a wider audience. You can increase your visibility and attract potential buyers by utilizing social media platforms, email marketing, and other online tools. Additionally, partnering with influencers or other sellers can help you expand your reach and attract new customers.

In conclusion, staying up-to-date with trends in foot picture aesthetics is essential for women and female foot models looking to sell foot pictures online. By understanding popular styles, editing techniques, and marketing strategies, you can create a successful business that attracts a broad audience and generates consistent sales. By continuously evolving and adapting to new trends, you can stay ahead of the competition and build a strong brand that resonates with your target market.

Chapter Nine

Soles of a Giant: Foot Model Nixie Kay

Unlike most foot models, I didn't just happen upon this career. Growing up, I had many nicknames. New girl, tall girl, big foot… It's easy to fall prey to bullies when you tower over your classmates, boys and girls alike. Being a lean and gawky, five foot-nine, thirteen-year-old makes you stand out like a sore thumb. Some of the many insults that stuck with me through the years were the comments about my giant feet. Some may say having a size 9 shoe size isn't that bad, and while I've grown accustomed to my long, slender feet, I still find myself wishing my feet were smaller. It wasn't until I started creating online content that I became aware that foot modeling and foot fetishes were a thing.

During a session on Onlyfans, a client asked me for a picture of my feet in a pair of high heels. I was very confused by this question as nobody had ever requested to see my feet before. He explained that he has a "giant woman foot fetish." He wanted me to tower over my camera like a giant and show him my heels. It seemed like a simple request, though, so I threw on some sexy high heels and snapped a few photos. From there, my foot modeling career took off. I had to learn how to care for my feet properly. Growing up with the lack of attention from a female role model left me uneducated in beauty and skincare. It wasn't until my early twenties that I learned that I should be moisturizing my skin daily. Exfoliation was a foreign word to me. I knew our skin could build up dead skin cells, but I was unaware I should be exfoliating it. The thought brings back a distant childhood memory of my father carving off the dead skin from his feet with a knife. I never really questioned it, and as I got older, I never realized I should've been taking better care of my skin.

What steps did you take to enter the industry?

After my encounter with the client asking for feet content, I began researching skincare techniques. I started advertising wherever I could and even got into selling my used socks. I grew to start loving my large feet, which were mercilessly made fun of for most of my teen years. I still find it surreal that some people find my soles sexy. Thanks to my newfound interest, my feet have been a recurring theme in written fictional fantasies and even featured at an art show in Seattle.

My biggest challenges were finding the correct skincare and finding the most successful places to advertise feet content. I initially started with TikTok; however, their community guidelines made it impossible to keep content up without getting reported. I grew quite a following and even though the content I posted was modest, my account was permanently banned within weeks. I then moved to Reddit, where my foot modeling career took off. People from all around the world wanted a piece of my soles. Even having clients ask to fly out to me to simply touch, smell, and see them in person. I never accepted those offers but it was still very flattering. Building a loyal client base is important for success in the fetish business. It's very lucrative to have returning clients, especially if you want to make a living in this line of work.

What are some common misconceptions about foot modeling, and how do you address them?

The most common misconception about foot modeling is that people assume it's easy. I mentioned earlier that I snapped a few quick photos of my feet in a pair of heels for a client. It wasn't as simple as that, though. I had to find the perfect pair of high heels to compliment my arches. I had to snap multiple photos from different angles, which was immensely difficult because all I had at the time was a cellphone, incapable of voice commands, and no timer. I also had to find the perfect lighting; at that time, all I had was a bedside lamp, and it was nighttime, so natural lighting was impossible. After a time, energy, and investing in my career, I was able to find proper lighting, better shoes, and a proper camera. It takes time to gain success in this industry, and it's not as simple as snapping a quick photo. Especially if you offer photo and video sessions to clients, they can be time-consuming and hard work.

In what ways does foot modeling intersect with other industries, such as fashion, beauty, movies, and even podiatry?

People often look down on foot models. Even though the fetish has been well known all over the world and throughout the history of time. People tend to overlook the symbolism in foot fetish even though it's included in modern television, the beauty industry, and fashion. Director Quentin Tarantino has always been well known for capturing the grace and beauty of feet in many of his films. Like any other part of the body, feet can be elegant.

Foot models are also hired to advertise for modern medical care. I recently sprained my ankle and have been doing a ton of research on how to properly heal. While reading, I came across many images of ankles and feet that were used to show how a healthy foot and ankle should look. Not every model in this business is in it for foot fetish reasons, but those who are shouldn't be judged for it. I've always found flat, wide feet fascinating and beautiful.

We all have our tastes. We all unabashedly love things that others may look down on but that doesn't mean that there is anything wrong with it. My advice for maintaining a career in foot modeling is to ignore the negativity. Don't allow others to bash you into hating what you do. Their opinion of your body and what you choose to do with it doesn't matter, your opinion of yourself does.

How did you balance showcasing your feet as a unique feature while maintaining your privacy and identity?

In the beginning, I did my best to maintain my privacy by not showing my face. I never showed my background either, as I have a large social media following and would instantly be recognized and outed. My family was unaware of my career choice, and I wanted to keep it that way. I use a stage name and only advertise on websites that protect my identity. A good source for advertising privately was Xbox. I changed my handle on certain games to "Buy My Feet Pics," and the amount of clientele I received was astounding. I also made sure to only game during school hours so that minors weren't adding me. When using sites that don't require age verification, always be sure to verify a client's age! I check identification before selling. Also, make sure to research your state laws around sex work.

What strategies do you use to navigate the competitive nature of the foot modeling industry, especially in marketing?

Foot modeling is an extremely competitive business. Everyone wants to do it because they feel it's easy but quickly give up when they realize that it's not. If you're unfamiliar with marketing strategies to advertise to the right crowd, then you will likely fail. You must be at the top of your game; you have to find the correct sites that work best for you. You must advertise often so that your content is always available. For example, if you are only advertising one day out of the week, then your post is going to get buried. There are thousands of people in the foot modeling business that advertise on every platform multiple times per day. If you only post once per day on one website, then it won't gain any traction or be seen. Consistency is key!

What advice would you give to those aspiring to follow a similar career path?

My last bit of advice would be to find others who are in this business and study their routine. Don't copy their work, just look for inspiration. If you see a cute pose that gained a lot of traction, then give it a try.

Make sure your feet are always well maintained. Moisturize daily, exfoliate weekly, take care of your nails and cuticles. If you can afford to, get a pedicure occasionally. Well maintained feet have a higher chance of success.

Don't be afraid to walk around outdoors barefoot though, some people enjoy a good muddy foot caught in nature! I'd also like to add that advertising and marketing are key to becoming successful. Set aside time each day for advertising. Make sure you're also taking time to take high quality photos. People don't want grainy, dark, hard to see images. Most importantly, have fun with it! Experiment with what works best for you and what makes you the happiest. My happiest is being the giant soled lady that people can look up to!

Chapter Ten

Ten Essential Tools for Aspiring Foot Models

Foot modeling has become increasingly popular in recent years, and it's no surprise why - after all, feet are considered one of the most attractive parts of the body. With the rise of social media platforms like Instagram and TikTok, foot modeling offers endless opportunities for aspiring models to showcase their unique talents and gain a following.

But before you start snapping pictures or filming videos of your feet, it is crucial to have the right tools at your disposal. Here are some essential items that every foot model should have:

Ring lights

1. Camera and tripod: Invest in a professional camera with high resolution and focus capabilities to capture stunning shots that impress clients. It is critical to create high- quality images that showcase the beauty and intricacies of your feet. The tripod provides stability when taking photos and reduces blurry or shaky pictures.

2. Light: Good lighting can make all the difference in a photo shoot. Consider investing in studio lights or ring lights specifically for photography purposes. This will ensure that your photos have perfect lighting every time.

3. Computer/laptop with internet connection

4. Editing Software

5. Cellphone

6. Stockings/Pantyhose

7. Socks

8. Various shoes, from high-heels, to boots and flats

9. Pedicures and a pedicure kit: To maintain beautiful toenails and cuticles, invest in a pedicure kit that includes nail clippers, a cuticle pusher, a foot rasp, a scraper, a callus remover, a cuticle remover, a foot file, a nail file, etc.

10. Basic foot care items: Invest in a good-quality foot cream to keep your feet soft, smooth, and camera-ready. Of course, as a foot model, it is essential to keep your feet well- maintained at all times

Chapter Eleven

Mark's Journey

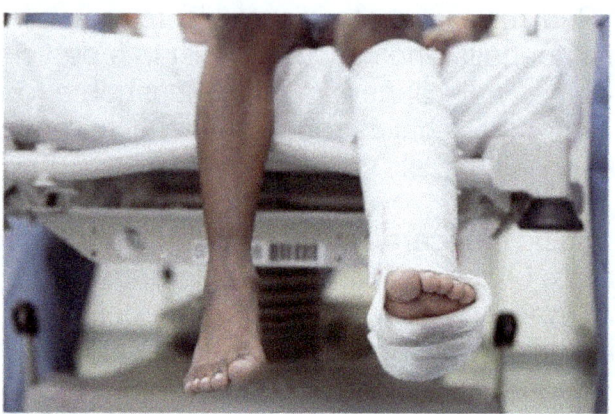

Growing up, I never paid much attention to my feet. They were there, carrying me from place to place without any fuss or complaints. That was, until I broke my leg when I was in the sixth grade—actually, I broke my foot. I was playing dodgeball and fell awkwardly. It was the first day of school, and we were there only for half a day. I visited the nurse and told her I thought I had broken my foot. Unfortunately, she didn't believe me. Now, here is my story:

On the first day of school, my friend Tyler and I exchange a grin, adrenaline already pumping through our veins. Dodgeball has always been our favorite—the thrill of dodging, ducking, and weaving, the satisfaction of landing a well-aimed throw. We've spent a few moments perfecting our technique, devising strategies to outmaneuver our opponents.

As we take our positions on the outside pavement, I feel a sense of normalcy wash over me. The familiarity of the game and the camaraderie with Tyler are comforting constants amid all the changes middle school brings. Little do I know that this ordinary game of dodgeball is about to take an unexpected turn, one that will test my resilience and shape the course of my journey in ways I never could have imagined.

"Nice one, Mark!" Tyler shouts as I manage to take out one of our opponents with a well-aimed throw. I flash him a grin, feeling the rush of adrenaline that comes with every successful hit.

I focus on the balls whizzing past, my mind wholly absorbed in the game. Each dodge feels like a small victory, and each throw is a chance to prove myself. The world narrows down to this moment, this game, this ball in my hands. I'm determined to give it my all, to push through the fatigue and the pressure, and come out on top.

The moment it happens is seared into my memory, a snapshot of pain and confusion I'll never forget. One minute, I'm running, dodging, fully immersed in the flow of the game. The next, I'm on the ground, a searing pain shooting through my foot like a bolt of lightning. It's unlike anything I've ever felt before, a white-hot agony that consumes my entire being.

"Mark!" Tyler's voice cuts through the haze of pain, tinged with concern. "Are you okay, man?"

I try to respond, but the words catch in my throat. I'm not okay, not by a long shot. This isn't just a simple twist or sprain. With a sudden and terrifying certainty, I know that something is seriously wrong.

"My foot," I manage to gasp out, my voice tight with pain. "I think it's broken."

The words hang in the air, heavy and ominous. I see the doubt in Tyler's eyes and the skepticism on the faces of my teammates and opponents alike. They think I'm exaggerating and just trying to get out of the game. But I know my body, and I know that this pain is real.

Nurse Grayson arrives on the scene, her kind face etched with concern. She kneels beside me, gently examining my foot. I wince at even the slightest touch, the pain intensifying with every passing second.

"It's probably just a sprain," she says, her voice soothing, but I'm unconvinced. "Let's get you to the nurse's office and take a closer look."

"Walk on it," she told me, thinking it was a sprain. So I walked on it as she asked. But with every step I took, the pain shot up my leg like a bolt of lightning. I insisted that something was wrong,

"See, you can walk on it. If you can walk on it, then it isn't broken. It's a sprain," she insisted. Yup, just as I thought, she didn't believe me and diagnosed it as a sprain.

"It's the first day of school and only a half day, so you

can wait. There is no need to leave early because everyone leaves early today," she said with a smile.

I want to argue, to demand that she listen to me, that she take my pain seriously. But I can see the resolve in her eyes, the unwavering belief that she knows best. With a heavy sigh, I nod, accepting the ice pack she offers me.

As I make my way back to class, each step sending shockwaves of agony through my foot, I can't help but feel a sense of betrayal. How could they not believe me? How could they dismiss my pain so easily?

But even as the doubts swirl in my mind, I cling to the certainty that I know my body. I know that this is more than just a sprain. The rest of the day passes in a haze of pain and frustration. Every step is a battle, every movement a reminder of the injury that no one seems to believe exists. My teachers look at me with concern, but I can see the flicker of doubt in their eyes, the unspoken question of whether I'm really as hurt as I claim to be.

I grit my teeth and push through, my determination fueling me even as my body screams in protest. I will not let them win, will not let their disbelief deter me from the truth I know in my heart or in my foot, actually.

As the final bell rings, I hobble towards the door, my mind already racing with thoughts of what comes next. I know that I cannot wait until tomorrow and cannot endure another day of this unrelenting pain. I need help, and I need it now.

By the time the last bell rang, I could barely walk. I hobbled home, trying not to cry with each step. My home was almost a mile away. Years later, when I Googled it, it was approximately .80 of a mile from Greenstreet Elementary School at 329 S 5th St, New Castle, IN 47362, to our house on New York Ave. I tell my friends that my leg is broken, but they don't believe me either.

"If your leg was broken, you wouldn't be able to walk on it. You have a sprained ankle, all it is," my friends chide me.

The journey home is an agonizing odyssey. Each step causes a searing bolt of lightning to shoot up my leg and ricochet through my entire being. I clenched my jaw, fighting back tears as I limped along the sidewalk, my backpack feeling like a lead weight on my shoulders.

Every inch of progress is hard-won, a battle against the relentless onslaught of pain that threatens to consume me. I can feel the curious stares of passersby, their eyes boring into me as I struggle onwards, but I refuse to meet their gaze, refusing to let them see the depths of my suffering.

"Just a little further," I whisper to myself, my voice barely audible over the pounding of my heart. "You can do this, Mark. You have to do this."

But with each passing moment, the pain grows more intense, more all-consuming. It's as if my foot is being crushed in a vise, the bones grinding together with every movement. I can feel the sweat beading on my forehead and the nausea rising in my throat as I fight to keep moving forward. But the journey seems endless, each step a Herculean effort that drains me of what little strength I have left. I can feel my resolve wavering, my determination flagging in the face of such overwhelming adversity.

"Almost there," I gasp, my voice little more than a ragged whisper. "Just a few more steps..."

When I finally make it home, my foot is swollen to twice its size. Unfortunately, I can't get inside the house because the door is locked. I don't have a key, so I have to wait until my older sisters get home with one to let me in. During my time waiting, I lay on the front porch. It was as if a dam had finally broken inside of me, the tears bursting forth with an unstoppable force, each one heavier than the last.

When my two older sisters arrive, I'm on my side, holding my foot and crying.

"Mark!" My sisters' voices ring out in unison. Their footsteps pound against the porch floor as they rush to my side. "What happened? Are you okay?

I try to respond, but the words catch in my throat, my breath coming in short, ragged gasps. I can feel their hands on my shoulders, their worried faces swimming in and out of focus as they try to help me up.

They immediately opened the door to help me get inside. Once inside, they call our mom.

"Mom!" one of them said, her voice laced with

urgency. "Mom, come home quick! Something's wrong with Mark!"

It seems like only moments later, I hear the screen door slam open, and then my mother is there, her gentle hands cradling my face as she tries to assess the situation.

"Mark, honey, what's going on?" she asks, her voice soft but insistent. "Talk to me, sweetheart. Where does it hurt?"

I manage to lift a shaking hand, pointing to my grotesquely swollen foot. "My foot," I gasp, my words punctuated by sharp intakes of breath. "It's broken, Mom. I know it is. I tried to tell them at school, but they wouldn't listen..."

My mother's eyes widen as she takes in the sight of my injury, her face paling with a mixture of shock and concern. "Oh, Mark," she breathes, her fingers gently probing the swollen flesh. "We need to get you to the hospital right away."

She turns to my sisters, her voice taking on a note of authority. "Girls, help me get your brother to the car."

As they carefully lift me to my feet, supporting my weight between them, I can't help but feel a sense of relief wash over me. Finally, someone believes me. Finally, I'm going to get the help I need.

But even as we make our way to the car, each step sending fresh waves of agony shooting through my body, I can't shake the feeling that this is only the beginning. The road ahead will be long and arduous, filled with challenges I can't imagine.

But for now, all I can do is hold on tight to my mother's hand and my sisters' steadfast presence at my side and hope that somehow, someway, I'll find the strength to keep moving forward.

The ride to the hospital is a blur of pain and anxiety, my mind racing with a thousand questions I'm afraid to ask. Will I need surgery? Will I ever be able to walk normally again? How long will it take to heal?

As we pull up to the emergency room entrance, my mother turns to me, her eyes filled with fierce determination. "Don't worry, Mark," she says softly, squeezing my hand in reassurance.

The next few hours pass in a whirlwind of activity, a seemingly endless parade of doctors and nurses poking and prodding at my injured foot. X-rays are taken, revealing the true extent of the damage - a break, the bone in my foot snapped in two.

As the doctor explained the diagnosis, his words washed over me in a daze. I couldn't help but feel a strange sense of vindication. I was right all along. My foot was broken like I'd been trying to tell everyone all day.

But even as they work to set the bone, encasing my foot in a bulky plaster cast, I can't shake the feeling that this is only the beginning of a much longer journey.

Well, that's my broken foot story. I had to wear a cast for the next eight weeks. Those eight weeks felt like an eternity.

I sat with my foot elevated during recess, watching my friends play without me. I gained an appreciation for the silent work my feet did every day. When the cast finally came off, I promised myself that if someone ever told me they broke some bone in their body, I would believe them.

It wasn't until I went through the Military Entrance Processing Station (MEPS) that my feet became a topic of interest again. Here is that story.

As I stood in line with other recruits, ready to begin our journey into the military, a medical officer took one look at my feet and exclaimed, "Wow! You have flat feet like I've never seen before."

My heart sank as he explained that having flat feet could disqualify me from certain positions in the military. He said that it may prevent me from even joining the military.

I didn't know what having flat feet meant, so I asked a recruit next to me. He laughed, saying, "It means you can ski without the skis!" From then on, I noticed how my feet (flat feet) differed from "regular" feet (feet with arches).

One day, while browsing at a bookstore, a book about reflexology caught my eye. Intrigued by the idea of using foot massage for relaxation and healing purposes, I purchased it and began practicing on myself.

To my surprise and delight, reflexology worked

wonders for relieving stress and tension in both mind and body. From curing a stomach ache to putting me to sleep, reflexology or a good foot massage worked wonders.

Foot Journey

Feet are a curious topic. From their often-overlooked role in our daily lives to the historical practices surrounding them, there's more to feet than meets the eye. My deeper foot journey into this world began with an academic pursuit—a college essay examining the harsh realities of Chinese foot binding. This brutal tradition sparked an outrage within me.

I reflected on my relationship with my feet as I delved into these painful practices. My past injury and flat arches made me acutely aware of their significance. Suddenly, feet weren't just a means of movement; they became a source of study that sparked my curiosity and led me down unexpected learning paths. Through my feet, I have gained insights into various cultures, practices, and perspectives and have come to appreciate their hidden complexity and significance in our everyday lives.

Fast forward to today, and it seems like everyone is talking about feet. They pop up in TV shows, commercials, movies—you name it! There's no denying that feet hold a unique place in popular culture and even draw interest from those who identify as having a foot fetish.

The Brutality of Chinese Foot Binding

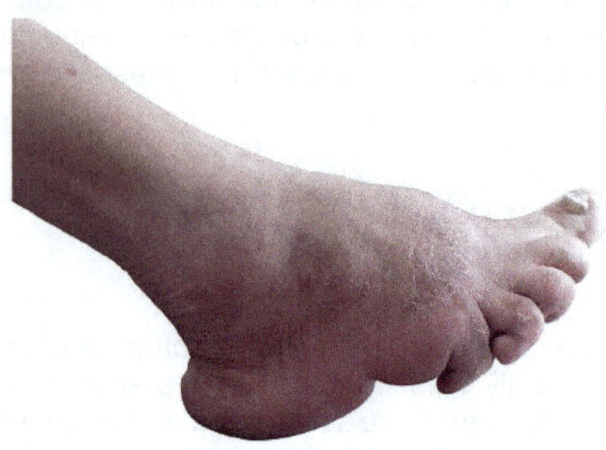

Writing my college essay on Chinese foot binding was an eye-opening experience. This gruesome practice, which aimed to achieve the ideal "lotus" foot, involved excruciating pain and lifelong consequences for women.

I immersed myself in historical accounts that revealed a world where beauty equated suffering. The process began in early childhood, with tiny feet tightly bound to prevent growth. The results were often debilitating deformities, including paralysis, gangrene, ulceration, or even death, though death was rare.

As I researched, I felt a mix of horror and shock. There was a tradition steeped in cultural significance yet so severe it silenced generations of women's voices. The practice was widespread during the Song Dynasty (960-1279). In the early 20th century, China finally ended it and made it illegal. However, some women still do it, and a few other countries do not outlaw it.

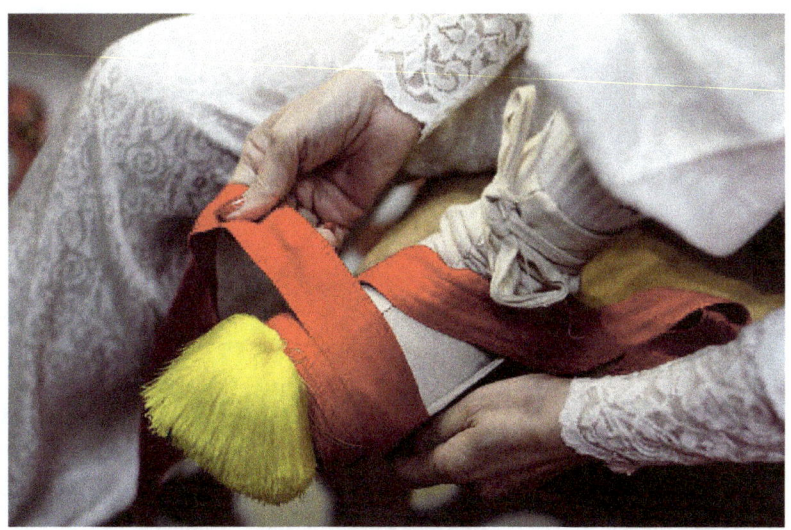

These stories illuminated resilience amid immense hardship, reminding me how societal standards may distort perceptions of beauty and worth. The men believed the bound foot was more attractive than an unbound foot. They thought it was the most intimate part of a woman's body. Some of them would drink liquid from a special shoe with a small cup in the heel. Others would drink directly from the shoe. Some men found the smell of the bound feet attractive. It was believed that the bound foot would transform the woman's body into a work of art, with the thighs becoming heavier and the vagina becoming tighter, a symbol of both beauty and submission.

This academic dive educated me about history and ignited questions about our modern ideals surrounding appearance, especially regarding something as fundamental as feet.

Feet are popular in the media

Feet have a significant presence in popular culture. They often serve as a focal point in various media formats, from TV shows to commercials and movies. Advertisers know that showcasing feet can evoke emotions and draw viewers' attention.

Think about it: What is typically highlighted when you see an ad for stylish shoes? The model's feet are elegantly adorned with the latest footwear. They catch your eye and entice you to imagine how those shoes would look on your feet.

Television programs frequently incorporate foot-related scenes, too. Whether it's a character getting pedicures or showing off their new sneakers, these moments resonate differently because of our inherent fascination with this part of the body. Most people didn't realize until recently that Nickelodeon's symbol was a foot. There were plenty of age-inappropriate foot jokes (and attire) on those shows. I'm sure some would argue that jokes about feet and farts will make most kids laugh. Others would say the scenes seemed more sexual than humorous.

Better Call Saul, *Suits*, and *Evil* are other TV shows that flaunt the feet. Going further back in time, in the hit TV show *Married with Children*, the lead character, Al Bundy, was a shoe salesman. In one episode titled T*he Agony of De-Feet*, Al had nightmares about feet and, in the dream, had to judge the ugliest feet in Chicago.

Movies also delve into themes surrounding feet—through dance sequences highlighting movement or romantic scenes where one partner gently caresses the other's foot. Or the camera angle starts at the feet poking out under covers and then slowly moves up to the couple kissing. Such portrayals deepen our connection to feet beyond mere functionality; they become symbols of beauty, intimacy, and even vulnerability.

The movie *Barbie* had a few foot-focused scenes. Many of Quentin Tarantino's movies include foot scenes, leading to reports of his foot fetish.

As we navigate daily life surrounded by images focused on feet, it becomes clear that this interest isn't merely superficial. It speaks volumes about cultural perceptions of beauty and identity while intertwining personal stories like my journey from injury and flat-footedness.

So next time you find yourself captivated by those perfectly manicured toes or striking heels on screen, remember there's more beneath the sole—a blend of history, artful representation, and individual experiences that shape our views on something as seemingly simple as…feet.

Photo Credits

The visual contributions from various sources enriched this book. Special thanks to Attorney Mark Nicholson, Jill Hills, and Nixie Kay for their invaluable images, which add a personal touch to the content. We also extend our gratitude to high-quality stock images that enhance the aesthetic appeal of our pages. The people shown in the book are models and were not involved in the writing of this book unless noted.

www.ingramcontent.com/pod-product-compliance
Lightning Source LLC
Chambersburg PA
CBHW050319230526
45471CB00005B/2257